# Apsley House
## The Wellington Collection

Julius Bryant

# CONTENTS

*Left:* The entrance hall
*Below:* A bronze statue
of Field Marshal Prince von
Blücher, Wellington's ally
against Napoleon, by
Christian Daniel Rauch
(1777–1857). It stands in
the entrance hall on a granite
base on loan from the Duke
of Wellington's family

*Facing page:* A detail of the
silver-gilt Portuguese service
on display in the state dining
room, with the Waterloo
Gallery glimpsed beyond

# Tour of Apsley House

### THE HOUSE

Apsley House is the product of two very different
styles of building and decoration. It was originally
built between 1771 and 1778 for Henry Bathurst,
1st Baron Apsley, after whom the house is still
named. He employed the fashionable architect
Robert Adam (1728–92) and the project was
one of only three large central London houses
both designed and furnished by Adam. The neat,
brick-built town house was completed in 1778
at a cost of £10,000. It was decorated in the
neoclassical style for which Adam was famed.
Although later alterations have obscured or
destroyed much of Adam's work, elements of
his original designs are still in place today.

In 1807 Apsley House was bought by
Marquess Wellesley, who had just returned from
India, where he had been Governor General. In
1817 the lease was purchased by his younger
brother Arthur Wellesley, the 1st Duke of
Wellington. Following the duke's victories over
Napoleon's forces, he had been granted £700,000
by the grateful nation. This was intended to help
construct a 'Waterloo Palace' for him and his heirs

in the country, which he chose not to build. The
duke later expanded Apsley House, employing the
architect Benjamin Dean Wyatt (1775–1855) to
enlarge and remodel the property. Wyatt's
alterations were on a grand scale, and included
refacing the entire house in Bath stone and adding
a massive extension. The house as it appears
today is largely a product of the 1st Duke's
refurbishments. In 1947 Gerald Wellesley, 7th
Duke of Wellington, generously gave the house
and collections to the nation.

### ■ ENTRANCE HALL

Stepping from the bustle of Hyde Park Corner into
the sudden calm of the hall today, visitors enjoy a
contrast that would have been appreciated in the
same way by the 1st Duke of Wellington's guests
and admirers. The roaring haste of the traffic is
muffled and then silenced by the closing door.
This entrance hall was created as part of the
remodelling carried out by the 1st Duke and his
architect, Benjamin Dean Wyatt, between 1828
and 1830. Adam's original front door had opened
into what is now the inner hall.

*Right:* The inner hall in about 1900, filled with sculpture
*Below:* The porter's chair still stands in the entrance hall

In Wellington's day, visitors entered under the suspicious gaze of a footman, whose draught-proof porter's chair can still be seen. Those who came as Wellington's admirers, with no claim on his time, might be shown no further than the 'Museum', the room off the entrance hall, which still contains displays of the duke's memorabilia and victory gifts. Acquaintances of the duke might hope to be directed to the chairs in the inner hall to wait. Business callers, however, might remain in the entrance hall making use of the six chairs, the table 'with oilcloth cover' and the 'bronze umbrella stand', protected against the draught of the opening door by the 'high six-fold screen covered with scarlet cloth and mouldings', described in an inventory of 1854.

No paintings or sculptures are recorded here in the 1st Duke's day but by 1857 his son had installed busts of King George III, Prince Albert and the 1st Duke of Wellington; by 1882, classical busts of Cicero, Athena and Septimius Severus, together with a modern bust of Alexander the Great and a statue of Eros, had been added. Wellington's functional entrance hall had become the first room of a sculpture gallery that leads into the 1st Duke's display in the inner hall. The bronze statue on a carved granite pedestal represents the Prussian Field Marshal, Prince von Blücher, and was placed here by Wellington as a memorial to his friend and ally against Napoleon. It is a copy by Christian Daniel Rauch (1777–1857) of a monument by the same artist, formerly at Breslau, Germany, that Wellington saw unveiled in 1826.

## 2 INNER HALL

This was the original entrance hall of the house, which Adam called the 'Anti-room'. A survey of 1828 describes it as 'paved with Portland Stone … with a Valet's Room and closet on the east side'. Stairs to the basement now fill the site of the closet but the 'Valet's Room' continues in use as the manager's office. The duke displayed an impressive collection of marble busts in this room. The three French mahogany Empire-style side tables with granite slab tops, made in about 1810 (on loan from the Duke of Wellington's family), were also here. The present Minton mosaic tile floor and cast-iron radiator covers were probably installed in about 1860. The mahogany doors date from between 1828 and 1830 when Wyatt converted Adam's entrance hall. The paintwork, imitating marble and stone blocks, is a re-creation from 1995.

Cutaway view
of Apsley House

1 Entrance hall
2 Inner hall
3 Principal staircase
4 Piccadilly Drawing Room
5 Portico Drawing Room
6 Waterloo Gallery
7 Yellow Drawing Room
8 Striped Drawing Room
9 Octagon Passage
10 State dining room
11 Slip passage
12 The Museum

*Above right: The plasterwork ceiling in the stairwell is decorated with a 'W' beneath a ducal coronet. It does not appear in Wyatt's original design and must have been added at Wellington's request*
*Below: Bust of Wellington by Benedetto Pistrucci, 1832*

*Facing page:* Napoleon as Mars the Peacemaker *by Antonio Canova, 1802–6*

## 3 PRINCIPAL STAIRCASE

Entering the stairwell, visitors encounter one of the most extraordinary works of art in Britain, the colossal marble statue *Napoleon as Mars the Peacemaker* by the Italian sculptor Antonio Canova (1757–1822). Today the sculpture may prompt smiles because of its nudity, but to the sculptor, then the leading artist in Europe, this was a work of great integrity.

Commissioned by Napoleon during his period as First Consul, Canova sought to emulate the example of Antique emperors, who were shown as gods in ideal nude form. Canova's sculpture was carved from a single block, with the exception of the left arm, and was finished in Rome in 1806. But it did not arrive in Paris until 1811, by which time Napoleon was Emperor. By then in his early forties, he preferred a more modest self-image. Declaring it to be 'trop athlétique', Napoleon insisted Canova's masterpiece remain covered up in the Louvre. After Waterloo, Canova endeavoured to buy the sculpture back but in 1816 the British Government bought it for 66,000 francs and the Prince Regent (later King George IV) presented it to the Duke of Wellington. Wellington could hardly refuse such a gift. He admired Napoleon and acquired several portraits of him. The stairwell was the only possible location for the sculpture at Apsley House. Even so, the

floor underneath the statue had to be reinforced with a brick pillar to support its great weight.

Robert Adam's plans of 1771 reveal that the stairs originally rose from the ground to first-floor level behind columned screens and went no further. The present recasting of the room dates from Wyatt's modifications in 1829, by which stage the Canova sculpture was already in place. The ceiling plasterwork also dates from this time and includes a 'W' beneath a ducal coronet; as it does not appear in Wyatt's original design, this detail must have been his client's contribution.

Behind the closed doors facing the statue a secondary staircase links the basement to the upper floors of this five-storey house. The other pair of doors leads to the 1st Duke's library. Today both sets of doors lead to the private apartments of the present Duke of Wellington and his family.

## 4 PICCADILLY DRAWING ROOM

This room was one of Adam's finest interiors for the house, and his chimney piece, ceiling and frieze still survive. The room now presents the taste of the 1st Duke of Wellington and Benjamin Dean Wyatt, following their modification and redecoration of the house between 1828 and 1830. A plan by Robert Adam shows this room with an alcove entrance, a screen of two columns across the curved end and niches flanking the

*Above:* Rossini and Paganini
accompanying the Italian
soprano Giuditta Pasta,
engraved by Joseph McGuire,
c.1832; Madame Pasta was
one of five singers
accompanied by Rossini at
a private concert at Apsley
House on 24 June 1824
*Right:* Chelsea Pensioners
Reading the Waterloo
Despatch, 1816–22, by
David Wilkie (1785–1841)

*Facing page:* The Piccadilly
Drawing Room

### The Waterloo Despatch

On the wall opposite the windows hangs the painting by David Wilkie, *Chelsea Pensioners Reading the Waterloo Despatch.* Outside Chelsea Hospital, on 22 June 1815, a Chelsea Pensioner reads aloud the *Gazette of Waterloo*, the official account of victory over Napoleon. Among some 50 figures there are more than 15 character studies, including a black dog known as 'the Old Duke', which followed the Blues regiment through Spain.

Wellington commissioned this painting in 1816, the year after Waterloo, as 'a parcel of old soldiers … at some public-house in the King's Road, Chelsea'. He must have intended it as a tribute to his troops, in the manner of the anecdotal Dutch genre paintings he was buying in Paris at that time, many of which still hang in this room today. This was Wellington's most expensive painting: he paid Wilkie £1,260 for it. When it was exhibited at the Royal Academy in 1822, hung next to Sir Thomas Lawrence's portrait of the duke, a rail had to be installed to keep the jostling crowds at bay. In 1841, Wellington bought (for £525) *The Greenwich Pensioners Commemorating Trafalgar*, which had been painted between 1818 and 1835 by John Burnet, on speculation. This painting also hangs in this room.

fireplace. Wyatt replaced the niche to the left of the fireplace with a doorway when the new state dining room was built in 1820, to provide access between these two rooms. The niche to the right of the fireplace was probably removed at the same time.

The Italian composer of operas Giacchino Rossini performed at Apsley House on 24 June 1824, accompanied by the star opera singer Madame Pasta. Their recital was probably given in this room, and Rossini may have performed on the zebrawood octagon piano, made by Pape of Paris and London, which survives in the Duke of Wellington's family collection. An inventory of 1854 records the furniture in the Piccadilly Drawing Room, including a central square ottoman (a four-sided sofa), another ottoman fitted to one corner of the room, two bookcases in rosewood and Boulle (brass and tortoiseshell) and two card-tables, also in rosewood and Boulle. The present restoration of Wyatt's decorative scheme dates from 1980, when the walls were hung to recreate the yellow striped 'tabaret' (a silk satin fabric) as described in the 1854 inventory.

*Right:* Hyde Park Corner photographed from the air in the 1930s, showing Apsley House at the end of a row of houses along Piccadilly. It was known as 'No.1 London', as it was the first house on Piccadilly

*Below:* Achilles in the Sulks by Thomas Howell Jones, 1827, showing Wellington after he had resigned as Commander-in-Chief, with the Achilles statue outside the window

*Bottom:* Achilles by Richard Westmacott, unveiled in honour of Wellington by the women of Britain in 1822

## THE SETTING

From the windows of the Piccadilly Drawing Room, visitors can appreciate the setting of Apsley House, standing on Piccadilly, at the formal entrance to Hyde Park. To the south and east lie Buckingham Palace, its walled gardens and Green Park. When Apsley House was first built, this fashionable Mayfair location was right on the western edge of London, with fine views of the surrounding parks. Although there was a great deal of building nearby from the 18th century onwards, it was not until 1962 that Apsley House was isolated in its current position, when Park Lane was diverted to Hyde Park Corner and the houses immediately to the east of Apsley House were demolished, cutting it off from Piccadilly.

### Wellington Arch and Hyde Park Screen

The house nonetheless retains some of the grandeur of its original setting, in the various monuments and sculptures that surround it. The Piccadilly Drawing Room gives a good view of the Wellington Arch, which can also be visited. Erected between 1827 and 1828 by the architect Decimus Burton (1800–1881), it originally stood in line with the present Hyde Park Screen (immediately to the west of Apsley House), created at the same time by the same architect, to form a grand entrance to Buckingham Palace gardens and Green Park from Piccadilly. Burton intended it to be decorated with

sculpture celebrating the defeat of Napoleon, but the project ran over-budget and only some of the carvings were in place by the time work finished in 1830. By 1838, plans were underway to place on top of the arch a statue in honour of the Duke of Wellington. The final design, a giant bronze equestrian statue of the duke, was installed, despite controversy, in 1846. Rows over the statue continued unabated, and in 1883, when the arch was moved to its present position to ease traffic congestion at Hyde Park Corner, the statue was dismantled. It was moved to the military training school at Aldershot, Hampshire, where it remains. In 1888, another statue of Wellington was unveiled opposite Apsley House to replace the giant equestrian statue. This was designed by Sir Joseph Edgar Boehm (1834–90).

### Marble Arch

While the Wellington Arch was being built, another arch to commemorate Britain's victories in the Napoleonic Wars was being planned by the architect John Nash. It was to stand outside Buckingham Palace, which Nash was working on at the time. Due to disputes and financial difficulties, Marble Arch, completed in 1833, was much more modest than the original designs. It was moved to its present location at the north end of Park Lane in 1850–51, to allow for an extension to Buckingham Palace.

## Commemorative Statues

A more personal tribute can be glimpsed from the window of the state dining room in winter, when the trees have lost their leaves. The bronze statue of *Achilles* by Richard Westmacott (1775–1856), standing in Hyde Park, was raised in honour of the Duke of Wellington in July 1822. Funded entirely by British women, the naked figure, cast from captured cannon, was soon nicknamed 'the Ladies' Fancy Man'. Britain's first outdoor nude statue, it caused considerable debate. Predating the Marble Arch and the Wellington Arch, it was the first of several monuments erected nearby to honour individual participants in the wars against the French. Frederick Augustus, Duke of York and Commander-in-Chief of the army from 1798 to 1809 and 1811 to 1827, had a statue erected to him in 1834. Wellington chaired the public meeting to inaugurate the fund for the memorial. The statue was designed, like *Achilles*, by Richard Westmacott; it stands in Waterloo Place on a granite column by Benjamin Dean Wyatt. Nelson's Column, erected in Trafalgar Square in 1843, supports a statue by E H Baily of the hero of Trafalgar. Again, Wellington presided over the plans for the memorial, combining the statue with a column designed by William Railton. A less

martial statue was unveiled at the south end of Park Lane in 1880, to Lord Byron. The bronze statue by Charles Belt shows the poet with his dog, Bo'sun.

## World War Memorials

Memorials to more recent conflicts have joined the Wellington statue and Arch around the Hyde Park Corner traffic island. Two First World War memorials were erected in 1925: the Royal Artillery Memorial, designed by Charles Sargeant Jagger and Lionel Pearson, and the Machine Gun Corps Memorial by Francis Derwent Wood. The Memorial Gates, designed by Liam O'Connor and erected at the top of Constitution Hill in 2002, honour troops from Africa, the Caribbean and the Indian sub-continent, while the Australian War Memorial of 2003, designed by the artist Janet Laurence and the architects Tonkin Zulaikhan Greer, commemorates losses in both world wars. The memorial to New Zealand's losses in the two world wars, by the architect John Hardwick-Smith and the sculptor Paul Dibble, consists of 16 bronze 'standards'. It was dedicated in 2006. The RAF Bomber Command memorial in Green Park was designed by Liam O'Connor and Philip Jackson in 2012.

*Above: The Wellington Arch in about 1860, with the giant bronze figure of the duke designed by Matthew Cotes Wyatt (brother of Benjamin Dean Wyatt, Wellington's architect for Apsley House)*
*Below: The Royal Artillery Memorial at Hyde Park Corner*
*Below left: Apsley House and Hyde Park Screen, photographed between 1890 and 1900*

## **5** PORTICO DRAWING ROOM

This room takes its present name from the Corinthian portico added to the exterior of the house in 1828, when Benjamin Dean Wyatt encased the brick building in Bath stone. Identified by Robert Adam as the '2nd Drawing Room', this room was originally designed to make the most of the house's exceptional setting. Before Wellington and Wyatt added the Waterloo Gallery, the wall facing the fireplace would have afforded a fine prospect out across Hyde Park from three windows. Facing west, the room would have been filled with sunlight in the afternoon and, as the south wall was solid, none of the noise from Piccadilly would have intruded on the illusion of a country-house saloon. At night, candlelight shone from gilded candelabra on *torchères* decorated with seated griffins, designed to match the original pier glasses. The tall windows under the portico were only created in 1828, together with the vast pier glasses (which are today on loan from the Duke of Wellington's family), to compensate for the removal of the windows in the west wall, when the Waterloo Gallery was installed.

A further clue to the character of the original room can be found in the fine marble chimney piece, which was probably carved by John Deval the Younger (1728–94). Adam's design includes an ornament of stags, a quote from the coat of arms of his patron Baron Apsley, later 2nd Earl of

Bathurst. The actual chimney piece is decorated with a frieze of Cupid and Psyche, and with symbols of seduction: a quiver of Cupid's arrows crossed with a flaming torch of passion. This romantic theme continues in Adam's surviving ceiling and frieze, and suggests that he may originally have intended this room as a ladies' drawing room. The pier glasses, overmantel and pier tables were designed for the room by Wyatt, and four more 'handsome carved and gilt tables', possibly also designed by Wyatt, are mentioned in the earliest known inventory of the room, drawn up in 1854. These side tables would have given the room a more formal character.

The present colour scheme, hangings, curtains and carpet date from 1978 and 1995 and are a re-creation by the Victoria and Albert Museum of the decoration as it survived in 1852. Paintings in the room from the duke's day include portraits of prime ministers (Pitt the Younger and Spencer Perceval), Napoleon and Marshal Soult, the leader of the French forces against Wellington in Spain. A portrait of Charles Arbuthnot (1767–1850), also hung in this room by Wellington, commemorates the 15 years during which the two men resided together at Apsley House. Wellington was an ardent admirer of his friend's wife, Harriet Arbuthnot, and after her sudden death in 1834, aged 40, from cholera, Wellington invited Charles to live out his days at Apsley House. The large copies after Raphael (on loan from the Duke of Wellington's family) were commissioned by the 1st Duke when he was in Paris, as Commander-in-Chief of the Allied Armies of Occupation in France, from the chief conservator at the Louvre, Féréol Bonnemaison. Wellington ensured the safe return of the original paintings to the Prado in Madrid, together with other masterpieces from conquered countries that Napoleon had sought to keep in Paris. The magnificent pair of Sèvres porcelain vases, made in 1814, are recorded in this room in 1853. They are decorated with a quagga and a gnu, animals copied from Samuel Daniell's engravings of African scenery and animals published in 1804. Each vase stands on an ormolu (gilt-bronze) foot by the celebrated goldsmith Pierre-Philippe Thomire (1751–1843).

A painting by William Salter (on loan from the Duke of Wellington's family) records the Waterloo Gallery in use for the Waterloo Banquet of 1836. It shows Wellington proposing the loyal toast, prior to the Grenadier Guards playing the national anthem and the guests settling into dessert. The women of the party appear only in the doorway – they were not present during the banquet but were admitted for the speeches

*Above:* The Waterloo Banquet, *by William Salter, 1836 (on loan from the Duke of Wellington's family)*
*Below:* Napoleon Bonaparte *(1769–1821), a portrait by Robert Lefèvre, 1812*

## 6 WATERLOO GALLERY

This is one of the great palatial interiors of Britain. More than 28m (90ft) long, the magnificent gallery fills two storeys and stretches beyond the back of the original house by two window bays in its own extension built between 1828 and 1829.

The Duke of Wellington had several reasons for creating such an impressive space. The main purpose of the gallery may have been to accommodate the Waterloo Banquet, an annual dinner held at Apsley House to celebrate the defeat of Napoleon. In the early years, before the Waterloo Gallery was created, Wellington hosted a select gathering; in 1821, for example, the guest list included King George IV, most of the royal dukes and foreign ambassadors, and Wellington's own generals who had fought with him at Waterloo. Rather than see the numbers of veteran generals dwindle with the passing years, Wellington expanded his guest list to include those younger officers present at the battle who later rose to the same rank. The Waterloo Gallery could seat 85 for ceremonial banquets. King William IV was guest of honour in 1830 and the dinner continued annually until the duke's death in 1852.

The Waterloo Gallery also raised Apsley House from an aristocratic town house to palatial status, befitting the foreign princes and politicians the duke received here. The architectural style of the room evokes the age of King Louis XIV of France, in preference to the Greek Revival that succeeded Adam's influence, the French Empire style favoured by Napoleon, or the Egyptian Revival that followed Napoleon's campaign to the Nile. The windows in the Waterloo Gallery have sliding shutters fitted with mirrors, which can be pulled across the windows at night. The light from the *torchères* and central chandelier would have flickered over gilded decoration and silk hangings, reflected by the mirrored shutters, evoking Louis XIV's Versailles and its celebrated mirrored room known as the *Galerie des Glaces* (created between 1678 and 1685 by the French architect J H Mansart). Wellington must have wished to share with his guests some of the splendours of the *ancien régime*, befitting his title as Prince of Waterloo and his position as a former Commander of the Allied Forces of Occupation in France, responsible for restoring Louis XVIII to the French throne. But the Waterloo Gallery gives only a pale reflection of Wellington's ambitious architectural plans. He had been

*Below left: A watercolour painting of the Waterloo Gallery in 1852 by Joseph Nash, which records the denser arrangement of paintings and the yellow silk damask covering the walls at that time*

*Facing page: View of the Waterloo Gallery, showing the sliding shutters fitted with mirrors*

'I am rather discontented, however, for I think he is going to spoil his gallery &, as I took infinite trouble about it, it vexes me …. He is going to hang it with yellow damask, which is just the very worst colour he can have for pictures & will kill the effect of the gilding. However, he will have it.'
Mrs Arbuthnot, writing about Wellington in 1828, shown here in a miniature after a portrait by Sir Thomas Lawrence

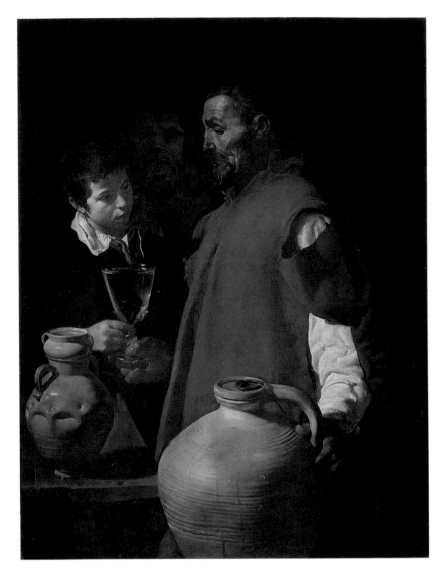

*Above:* The Waterseller of Seville *by Diego Velázquez, c.1620*

*Right:* Two Young Men Eating at a Humble Table, *by Diego Velázquez, c.1618–20*

building and upkeep of a Waterloo Palace would have ruined him and his heirs, and so restricted himself to remodelling Apsley House. His country residence at Stratfield Saye proved adequate for his needs.

The Waterloo Gallery provided a fitting home for most of the 165 paintings from the Spanish Royal Collection. They had been discovered after the Battle of Vitoria in 1813 in the abandoned baggage carriage of Joseph Bonaparte, brother of Napoleon and at that time king of Spain. The Duke of Wellington was given the paintings by King Ferdinand VII of Spain in 1816.

Many details in the Waterloo Gallery, including the gilded overdoors, were designed by the duke's close friend Mrs Arbuthnot. She was asked to intervene in November 1828, when relations between Wellington and Wyatt became strained.

In March 1830 Wellington insisted on hanging the gallery with yellow damask, which Mrs Arbuthnot thought was the worst colour for paintings. It seems unlikely that the yellow clashed with the paintings given the density of the duke's arrangement. As he hung more than 130 paintings in the room (almost double the 70 here today) they would have been as closely packed as the paintings in the Piccadilly Drawing Room today. The 1st Duke was simply following the Regency taste for yellow walls. He would have seen gilding and yellow silk used together in India and Russia and had chosen it for three other rooms in this suite. The effect of the yellow wall-coverings in the Waterloo Gallery is recorded in a watercolour painted by Joseph Nash in 1852 (see page 15). Nevertheless, the 2nd Duke of Wellington replaced the yellow silk damask with red almost immediately after his father's death.

Nash's painting also shows the two vast *torchères*, made of grey Siberian (Korgon) porphyry. They were originally intended for the Winter Palace in St Petersburg but were presented to the duke in 1826 by Tsar Nicholas I of Russia. For the Waterloo Banquet the tables were assembled around them, and the two vases of Swedish porphyry were dressed with flowers. These vases were presented by King Charles John XIV of Sweden and are on loan from the Duke of Wellington's family. Nash's watercolour also shows a bordered carpet, described in an inventory of 1854 as 'a large cut pile carpet to centre of room', together with 'a ditto a size smaller for each end'.

expected to build at Stratfield Saye in Hampshire a magnificent Waterloo Palace, the 19th century's answer to Blenheim (the palace in Oxfordshire created by Sir John Vanbrugh from 1705 for the 1st Duke of Marlborough as a national gift after his victory over the army of King Louis XIV of France). But Wellington must have realized that the

*Far left:* Portrait of Pope Innocent X, *by Diego Velázquez, 1650*
*Left:* Portrait of a Man, Probably José Nieto, *by Diego Velázquez, c.1635–45*
*Below:* The Agony in the Garden *by Antonio Allegri, known as Correggio, c.1523–4*

# The Spanish Royal Collection

*Wellington was given many masterpieces from the Spanish Royal Collection by a grateful King Ferdinand*

Acquired as rolled-up canvases, the paintings gradually covered the walls as more and more were conserved and framed each year. Most of the works are relatively small for a gallery of this scale, suggesting that Joseph Bonaparte's hurried selection must have been influenced by their portability.

The greatest masterpieces in the collection today are four paintings by Diego Velázquez (1599–1660) – *The Waterseller of Seville*; *Two Young Men Eating at a Humble Table*; *Portrait of a Man, Probably José Nieto*; and *Pope Innocent X* – together with *The Agony in the Garden* by Correggio (about 1494–1534). The President of the Royal Academy, Benjamin West, thought the Correggio was worth fighting a battle for, and that it should be framed in diamonds. Wellington had all the paintings framed in the rococo revival taste appropriate to the room. He had a special frame made for his favourite painting, the Correggio, with a locking glass window on hinges. Wellington kept the key in his pocket and would lend it to no one. He was apparently in the habit of raising the window to dust the painting with his own handkerchief.

*Right:* View through the Yellow
Drawing Room towards the
Striped Drawing Room
*Far right:* Adam's design for
Lady Bathurst's watch case
*Below:* Head of a Dancer,
a marble bust by Antonio
Canova, given by the sculptor
to Wellington in 1817

*Watch Case for Lady Bathurst*

### 7 YELLOW DRAWING ROOM

The second door in the Waterloo Gallery leads
back into the original house, built by Adam. In
Adam's plan this room is called simply the '3rd
Drawing Room or Toillet Room'. His original
marble fireplace still survives, together with some
of his designs for the fittings and furnishings of the
room, including one drawing for a table frame and
top and another for an exquisite watch case for
Lady Bathurst, a personal trophy to fashion where
her watch could luxuriate overnight. In the 1st
Duke's day this room was used as a drawing room.
By 1854 furnishings included a 'Grecian Couch in
white and gold', 11 chairs, four footstools, a writing
table, a sofa table, lamps and six stuffed birds on a
stand. Striped 'tabaret' silk decorated the walls, with
amber silk damask curtains. The present decoration
is a reconstruction from 1994.

The bust by Antonio Canova (on the pier table)
was a gift to Wellington from the sculptor in 1817.
It is one of four 'ideal' heads presented by Canova
to the British gentlemen who were instrumental in
returning to Rome treasures looted by Napoleon
for the Louvre. Canova had begun the repatriation
of such booty by requesting the return of the Papal
archives to the Vatican, so that daily business might
continue. As Commander of the Allied Armies of
Occupation in France, Wellington was forced to
begin a more widescale denuding of the 'Musée
Napoleon' after the king of the Netherlands
decided to send his troops into the Louvre to
recover his country's stolen masterpieces.

### 8 STRIPED DRAWING ROOM

In the original house designed by Robert Adam, a
dressing room, a servant's room and a bedroom
completed the circuit of fine rooms on the first
floor. Wyatt combined these three rooms to
make the present Striped Drawing Room at the
same time as the addition in 1820 of the state
dining room that lies beyond, thus providing
Wellington with a room where his guests could
relax, before or after dinner, and where the duke
could also display his growing collection of
portraits. Card tables covered with green cloth
were provided, for playing loo and *écarté*, together
with a board for draughts and backgammon, ivory
dice boxes and table lamps. This room also
became a personal hall of fame to Wellington's
military friends. The idea may date from his visit to
St Petersburg in 1826, where he would have seen
the gallery that Tsar Nicholas I was building in his

Winter Palace for portraits of heroes of the Napoleonic Wars. The three full-length portraits by Sir Thomas Lawrence, still on display in the room today, were planned as part of a series, but after the artist died the duke had to resort to buying pictures by other artists to complete his gallery of military heroes.

The distinctive character of the interior comes from the striped hangings and furniture, originally installed in 1826 (the current hangings are reproductions). Here Wyatt and Wellington might have been inspired by the celebrated tent room in Napoleon's apartment at Malmaison, the house near Paris decorated between 1800 and 1802 for Joséphine Bonaparte by architects Charles Percier and Pierre-François-Léonard Fontaine. Describing the effect of the room in 1853, as well as the portraits of politicians and of Napoleon in the Portico Drawing Room, the *Quarterly Review* likened it to a 'private Valhalla', the heavenly hall of Viking mythology where the bravest warriors were immortalized.

To accompany the portraits of his friends, Wellington bought the panoramic painting *The Battle of Waterloo* (1843) by Sir William Allan (1782–1850; illustrated on pages 30–31).

*Above left:* The Striped Drawing Room painted in 1852 by Thomas Shotter Boys
*Left:* Sir Thomas Lawrence's portrait of Henry William Paget, 1st Marquess of Anglesey, who served with Wellington at Waterloo
*Below:* Portrait of Field Marshal Prince von Blücher by George Dawe, 1818. Blücher's arrival at the Battle of Waterloo with the Prussian army at 5pm ensured the defeat of Napoleon

When Wellington saw this painting exhibited at the Royal Academy he remarked, 'Good, not too much smoke,' and reserved it for his collection. Today it still hangs where he left it, as recorded in a watercolour of the room painted by Thomas Shotter Boys in 1852 (see page 19).

The painting shows the battle from the point of view of the French Army, at 7.30pm on 18 June 1815. Napoleon can be seen in the foreground at the right of the picture, mounted on his white charger, while Wellington is a tiny figure in the middle distance to the left, on his faithful chestnut, Copenhagen. At this stage in the battle, things had begun to swing against the French forces, despite their numerical superiority to the combined British, Prussian, Dutch and Belgian troops, jointly commanded by Wellington and the Prussian Field Marshal, Prince von Blücher. This was Napoleon's last offensive, when he sent five of his battalions against the centre of the allied position. But the battle was to last for only another half hour, ending in a massive rout of the French troops. Although Wellington displayed his usual sangfroid during the battle, he admitted afterwards, 'I never took so much trouble about any battle, and never was so near being beat.'

*Above: A portrait of Napoleon's sister Pauline Bonaparte, Princess Borghese, 1806, by Robert Lefèvre (1755–1830)*

*Right: Detail of the silver and silver-gilt Portuguese centrepiece on the table*

*Facing page: The state dining room, which was completed in 1819 by Benjamin Dean Wyatt. The annual Waterloo Banquet was held here until the Waterloo Gallery was finished ten years later*

## 9 OCTAGON PASSAGE

This magical little mirrored room, linking the Striped Drawing Room to the state dining room, has its modest name recorded in a floor plan drawn up by Wellington's architect, Benjamin Dean Wyatt, in about 1829. In Robert Adam's original plan the passage was not octagonal and it led to a 'Powdering Room' and closet off the adjoining bedroom.

## 10 STATE DINING ROOM

This grand dining room was finished in 1819 by Benjamin Dean Wyatt. Up to this point, the duke and his guests had dined downstairs. Wellington built his new state dining room as part of a three-storey addition to the north-east of Apsley House. Below were the duke's apartments; above, on the third storey, there were two bedrooms, all linked by new back stairs.

The state dining room was the setting for the great annual Waterloo Banquet from 1820 until the completion of the Waterloo Gallery ten years later. On its inauguration, this dining room must have seemed the ultimate expression of Wellington's ambitions to entertain in style. The arrangement of the room today gives some impression of the magnificence of the Waterloo Banquet.

The glittering centrepiece on display here is part of a silver and silver-gilt service presented to Wellington by the Portuguese Council of Regency in 1816, to commemorate victories over Napoleon in the Peninsular War (1808–14). In the centre, figures representing the four continents pay tribute to the united armies of Portugal, Britain and Spain while dancing nymphs encircle them. Battles are named on individual plaques. The full Portuguese Service comprises more than 1,000 pieces and was designed by the court painter Domingos António de Sequeira (1768–1857), and made at the artist's house from 1812 to 1816 by workers from the Military Arsenal in Lisbon.

An inventory also reveals that by 1854 this room had a carpet surrounded by an oil cloth (a forerunner of linoleum). Wellington would protect his carpets before the Waterloo Banquet by laying oil cloths and druggets (long woollen mats).

The state dining room was made for more than reunions of Waterloo veterans. With its state portraits, presented by the sitters themselves, it

*Right: The state dining room painted by Thomas Shotter Boys in 1852. This painting records on the dining room sideboard, flanking the empty support for the Wellington Shield, two equestrian statuettes, of Wellington and Napoleon, by Alfred, Count d'Orsay, 1845. Wellington claimed it was the image of himself that he most liked for posterity*

embodies Wellington's unique social position as the friend and near-equal of the crowned heads of Europe.

As Allied Commander, and a ready diplomat fluent in French, Wellington held a position that today might be equivalent to combining the duties of the commander of NATO with those of a roving ambassador. Yet however much he was revered and fêted abroad, back home in the decade after Waterloo, Wellington had no obvious role to play. His spell as Prime Minister (1828–30) proved how much his absence on military campaigns had left him out of step with the times and with growing calls for constitutional change.

Consciously or otherwise, Wellington seems to have created for himself in this almost windowless room a closed world commemorating old friends and the old order. Tact or modesty may have made it necessary to create the impression, preserved to this day, that the state dining room, and later the Waterloo Gallery, were created simply for an annual reunion of Wellington's comrades-in-arms from Waterloo, as if he had no more important guests or political agenda.

At the dinner table Wellington was reputedly an excellent host, putting his guests at ease with many humorous anecdotes. The novelist Walter Scott was surprised at his conversation, at 'the sweetness & abandon with which it flowed'. Wellington showed no interest in fine wines or food, however, eating little and swiftly, his favourite dishes being mincemeat, rice, or roast saddle of mutton with salad. To the frustration of his French chef, Wellington would simply return the proposed menu for the day without discussion, after scrawling across the bottom 'pudding and tart' to satisfy the demands of his sweet tooth.

## ▥ SLIP PASSAGE

Leaving the state dining room through the service door to the right of the sideboard, visitors enter the slip passage, which leads back to the Piccadilly Drawing Room. Behind the curved door from the state dining room lies another room (closed to visitors) that may have contained a water-closet for the convenience of dinner guests. The inventory of 1854 records dining tables stored in this passage ('2 butler tray stands' and 'Sundry deal tops and tressels used for the Gallery') with the floor covered by a fitted oil cloth to catch the spills. The cabinets are a modern addition to display pieces from the silver Portuguese Service. The tour continues downstairs in the Museum.

# The Waterloo Shield

*Inspired by the shield of Achilles described by Homer in* The Iliad

In 1822, the Merchants and Bankers of the City of London presented Wellington with a magnificent silver-gilt shield and a pair of candelabra to celebrate the victory at Waterloo, which had heralded a period of prosperity for the capital. The glittering Waterloo Shield was designed by Thomas Stothard in 1814 and made by Benjamin Smith; Smith also made the two Standard Candelabra between 1816 and 1817. The pieces were brought out for the annual Waterloo Banquet; when this took place in the state dining room they were displayed together on the sideboard. In 1822 James Deville invoiced the duke for 'fixing in the Sideboard … a Large Brass Plate with a Revolving mechanical joint … to attach the whole to the Shield to allow it to incline as may be required and to Revolve Round'. The shield and candelabra were usually displayed in the Museum, where they can still be seen today.

**Above:** *The Waterloo Shield shows Wellington in the central group with the 10 major battles from the Peninsular Campaign depicted in the surrounding reliefs*
**Left:** *Engraving, showing a detail of the Battle of Salamanca (1812) from the Waterloo Shield*

*Above: Three plates on display in the Museum, from the Saxon Service (top and bottom) and the Prussian Service (middle), depicting Apsley House before the extensive remodelling by the 1st Duke and Benjamin Dean Wyatt*

*Above right: The Museum painted in 1853 by Thomas Shotter Boys*

## 🄰 THE MUSEUM

After Waterloo Wellington was showered with gifts by monarchs grateful to him for saving their thrones from Napoleon. At Apsley House the duke created a private treasury, called the 'Museum', off the entrance hall to store and show to visitors these gifts. This was not a permanent display, for the silver and porcelain services and presentation plate came and went, dressing the tables of brilliant banquets hosted by Wellington upstairs.

The present room is the Museum's third location. Initially it stood on the site of the present entrance hall. When the west wing containing the Waterloo Gallery was added to the house between 1828 and 1830, the collection moved to the new sitting room beneath the gallery, at the north end of the wing, as recorded in two watercolours by Thomas Shotter Boys. The 2nd Duke of Wellington moved the Museum to its present position after his father's death in 1852, presumably in order to place it closer to the entrance for visitors. Shotter Boys recorded this arrangement in a watercolour of 1853 (above). The objects on display also proved inspiring for the Duchess of Wellington, who drew solace from the

collection during her last illness. During a visit to Apsley House on 24 April 1831, the novelist Maria Edgeworth encountered the duchess lying on a sofa admiring the trophies. This is a touching testimonial from a woman who spent much of her married life apart from her husband.

### Silver-gilt Plate Collection

The most eye-catching piece in the collection is the massive, glittering Waterloo Shield in its custom-built rosewood showcase, designed by Wyatt and Wellington (see page 23), flanked by the Standard Candelabra. These magnificent presentation pieces in gilded silver were intended for display together, blazing from the sideboard at the annual Waterloo Banquet. The case still contains the original mechanism by which the shield and candelabra can be rotated at the turn of a handle. After the shield and candelabra, the finest plate includes two silver-gilt centrepieces made by Paul Storr between 1810 and 1812 and the silver-gilt Waterloo Vase designed by Thomas Stothard and made between 1824 and 1825, each presented to Wellington by noblemen, gentlemen and officers. The Deccan Service was presented by officers who served in India in 1803.

### Egyptian Service

The porcelain on display nearly all dates from one decade, from about 1810 to 1820, and is of the highest quality. The Egyptian Service, displayed in the central case, was originally commissioned for Joséphine Bonaparte in 1809 to mark her divorce from Napoleon, but she rejected the gift in 1812. In 1818 King Louis XVIII of France presented the service to Wellington. The service was designed by Jean Charles Nicolas Brachard of the Sèvres porcelain factory. The designs for the 66 plates and other pieces were taken from illustrations of ancient Egyptian monuments in the celebrated book *Voyage dans la basse et la haute Égypte*, published in 1802 by Dominique Vivant Denon (1747–1825), following Napoleon's invasion of Egypt. In Wellington's own day, the Egyptian Service was kept in store.

### Prussian Service

The Prussian Service, displayed in cases on the south and east walls, presents Wellington's life and military campaigns in scenes painted on 64 dessert plates, as well as vases, ice-buckets, ice-cream pails and cups, fruit platters, sauce-boats, soup tureens and wine coolers. Made by the Berlin porcelain factory from 1816 to 1819, the service was presented to the duke by King Frederick William III of Prussia. The green porcelain obelisk, decorated with Wellington's titles and orders and flanked by white porcelain river gods, is one of 292 pieces from the service currently at Apsley House.

### Saxon Service

The Saxon Service was made from 1818 by the Meissen porcelain factory and presented to Wellington in 1819 by King Frederick Augustus IV of Saxony. Among 105 hand-painted dessert plates, two show views of Apsley House as it originally appeared, built in brick by Robert Adam (another plate depicting the house can be seen in the Prussian Service). The others are painted with scenes of battles and other views from the Napoleonic Wars. Only a selection from the service can be displayed; it also includes vases and sauce-boats.

*Left: Dinner plate from the Austrian Service*
*Below left: Large urn from the Prussian Service depicting the Battle of Waterloo*

### Austrian Service

The Austrian Service, the last great production of the Vienna porcelain factory, was presented by Emperor Francis II of Austria in 1820. The collection also includes 44 dessert plates in *gros bleu* Sèvres porcelain, painted between 1821 and 1822 and presented by King Louis XVIII of France in 1823.

### Swords and Batons

Other notable objects in the collection include 17 presentation boxes and a collection of 13 gold and silver swords, some used by the duke (including his sword from the Battle of Waterloo) and some captured from his opponents including the Indian leader Tipu Sultan of Mysore, and Napoleon himself. Napoleon's sword, made by his goldsmith Martin-Guillaume Biennais in about 1809, is displayed with a choice of three scabbards. It was intended for Napoleon's triumphal entry into Brussels but, legend has it, the sword was taken by a Prussian from Napoleon's carriage at Waterloo as he fled out the opposite door. The batons were presented to Wellington as commander of various European armies. Of the field marshal's batons, three are British, one Portuguese, one Hanoverian, one Dutch, one Spanish, one Austrian and one Prussian. They are accompanied by Wellington's staff as High Constable of England.

'[These are] all tributes to merit! There's the value; all pure, no corruption ever suspected even.' The Duchess of Wellington, talking about her husband's Museum in 1831, shown here in 1814 in a drawing by Sir Thomas Lawrence

*Right: A painting of 1840 by Andrew Morton (1802–45) showing Wellington in his library on the ground floor with his private secretary, John Gurwood*

**Below:** *The steward's room, photographed in 1949 when used as a store, long after domestic life at Apsley House had been interrupted by the Second World War*

## BASEMENT AND SERVANTS' QUARTERS

The basement of Apsley House was the domain of the servants, but it also accommodated ample stables and a coach house. A census of 1851 provides a glimpse of life below stairs, recording 13 male and eight female servants, including the steward (or butler), the housekeeper, two porters, two under-butlers, one footman, four housemaids, two kitchen maids, a stillroom maid, two coachmen, one groom and four 'helpers' in the stables (the cook is not recorded, so must have been away at the time of the census).

A floor plan from 1904 records more than 30 rooms within the basement, from the kitchen, scullery, larder, wine cellars, coal cellar and servants' hall to a carpenter's workshop and a large muniment room in which documents would have been archived. There was also a strongroom for the silver and silver-gilt dining services. At the centre of the basement a service staircase, opposite the principal stairs, ascends the full height of the house. This was the main thoroughfare for servants (who were expected to remain invisible

*Left*: The 1st Duke's study
shown in a watercolour by
Thomas Shotter Boys, 1852

to visitors), and also led to attic bedrooms where the under-servants slept, two or three to a room.

Wellington had his horses stabled at basement level, on the east side of the house. A steep ramp led down from a ground-floor stable block (now demolished) at the east end of the forecourt, to the stables court. At basement level, stables and a coach house were provided, while accommodation for grooms and coachmen occupied the ground floor. As the *Quarterly Review* noted in 1853, 'this basement-level courtyard proved particularly convenient for Wellington as he was able to mount and dismount, enter or leave a carriage, in secure privacy, free from the attentions of admirers and protesters'.

The main part of the basement open to visitors today is the former steward's room. It is last recorded as such in a state of abandoned disarray, in a photograph taken in October 1949 (see facing page). Other photographs taken at this time record a kitchen and secondary kitchen, a vegetable kitchen, a pastry kitchen and a servants' hall. The kitchen equipment was removed to the Museum of London shortly before Apsley House first opened as the Wellington Museum in 1952. At that time no

plans were made for showing the servants' quarters to the public. Today the basement gallery presents changing displays from the collections.

## PRIVATE ROOMS

The Wellington Museum Act of 1947, by which the 7th Duke gave the house and contents to the nation, reserved parts of the basement and the ground floor and all of the two top storeys for the Duke of Wellington and his family. They continue to live at Apsley House in these private apartments.

These rooms are not open to visitors, but their appearance in the 1st Duke's day is recorded in detailed descriptions and illustrations published in 1853, on the occasion of the first public opening by the 2nd Duke of Wellington. The thorough account of these rooms given by Richard Ford in the *Quarterly Review* in 1853 also appeared as the introduction to Ford's book *Apsley House and Walmer Castle* (London 1853) with illustrations taken from the watercolours of the interiors of the house specially commissioned from the artist Thomas Shotter Boys. These give a vivid picture of the house as it was arranged at about the time of the 1st Duke's death (see page 47).

# The Iron Duke's Career

## EARLY YEARS

Born in Dublin in 1769, the fourth son of the 1st Earl of Mornington, Arthur Wesley did not make a promising start. His father died when he was 12, and the same year he was sent to Eton, together with his younger brother Gerald. After three years, it was clear that Arthur was not doing well and his mother removed him from Eton, concluding that her 'ugly boy Arthur' was only good for cannon-fodder, or, as she put it, 'fit food for powder'. After she moved to Brussels in 1785, she enrolled Arthur in the École d'équitation, a military academy at Angers in France. Here Arthur gained his life-long fluency in French. After he left, his military career advanced, as was the custom, through the purchase of positions in regiments and he also entered the political arena as Member of the Irish Parliament for the constituency of Trim, from 1790 to 1795. By this time the family had changed its surname back to Wellesley, its 17th-century spelling.

## THE NAPOLEONIC WARS

Arthur Wellesley began his military career at a turbulent time in Europe. Instability had increased in the wake of the French Revolution of 1789, and in 1793 Napoleon led France to war against the British and their allies. Arthur saw his first action in the Netherlands in 1794, earning an official commendation for his part in an engagement against the French. In 1796, as a colonel, he sailed for India, another theatre of British military operations, discovering on the way that his brother had been offered an appointment as Governor General there. India was the making of Arthur as a military commander and civic administrator. In 1804, at the age of only 34, he achieved a victory that he would later consider his best battle, over the confederation of Maratha states at Assaye.

Returning to England in 1805, he was elected to Parliament the following year and appointed Irish Secretary. He also married, in 1806, Lady Catherine ('Kitty') Pakenham, daughter of Edward, 2nd Baron Longford. Arthur had known her in Ireland during the early years of his military career and had in fact proposed to her in 1793, when her family had put an end to the affair, disapproving of

his lowly prospects. It seems that Kitty had considered the engagement dissolved, but a mutual friend of the couple pressed Arthur to renew his proposals. Only a very strong sense of honour could have induced a notorious ladies' man, as Arthur already was, to agree to marry a woman he had not set eyes on for almost ten years. Apparently he regretted the match almost immediately, remarking to his brother at their wedding, 'She has grown ugly, by Jove!' It was not an easy marriage.

By 1807, Britain was in the middle of another military crisis. Napoleon had already defeated the Austrians, Russians and Prussians and Britain alone continued to hold out, having defeated the combined French and Spanish fleets at Trafalgar in 1805. Arthur Wellesley sailed for Denmark in 1807, to serve in an expedition against the Danish, culminating in the siege of Copenhagen. He performed creditably, and he was promoted to lieutenant-general and given command of 9,000 men when war with Napoleon flared up in Spain in 1808. This was the start of the Peninsular War (1808–14), triggered by a Spanish revolt against Napoleon when he deposed the king of Spain in favour of his brother, Joseph.

*Left:* The great portrait of Wellington by Francisco de Goya (1746–1828), now in the National Gallery; Goya completed the painting in 1812 but altered it in 1814 to show the extra honours his sitter had by then received

*Below:* Napoleon in the Prison of Nice in 1794, painted in 1841 by Edward Matthew Ward. Napoleon was placed under house arrest in 1794 because of his association with the revolutionary Robespierre. Wellington bought this painting directly from the artist in 1841

*Facing page:* Portrait of Wellington by Sir Thomas Lawrence, c.1814

*Above:* The Battle of
Waterloo, *painted in 1843
by Sir William Allan and
bought directly from him in
the same year by Wellington*

*Facing page: Some of
Wellington's battle orders
from the Battle of Waterloo*

## THE PENINSULAR WAR

Supported by the Spanish and Portuguese armies, the British troops had mixed fortunes in the Peninsular War, although Wellesley himself had some notable successes and was raised to the peerage as Baron Douro of Wellesley and Viscount Wellington of Talavera in 1809. For his capture of Ciudad Rodrigo in 1812 he was rewarded by Spain with the title of Duke of Ciudad Rodrigo and, following further successes that year, was appointed as *generalissimo* of the Spanish armies. Parliament rewarded him with a grant of £100,000; he was also elevated to marquess (August 1812) and awarded the Order of the Garter (March 1813).

The campaign of 1813 saw the French driven out of Spain and Wellington's advance into France.

After his victory at the Battle of Vitoria on 21 June 1813, Wellington was promoted to field marshal. Two days after facing Marshal Soult at the Battle of Toulouse (10 April 1814) Wellington learned that Napoleon had abdicated. He returned to England, after an absence of six years, and was created Marquess of Douro and Duke of Wellington, with a further grant voted by the House of Commons of £400,000. Six weeks later he was back in France as ambassador, and took up residence in Paris.

## THE WATERLOO CAMPAIGN

Napoleon's escape from exile on the island of Elba obliged Wellington to resume his military career, and in March 1815 he was appointed Commander of the Anglo-Netherland and Hanoverian forces in

Europe. Napoleon set out to defeat Field Marshal Prince von Blücher's Prussian army and then overcome Wellington's allied forces (only about a third of whom were British) before the Austrians and Russians could reach Belgium. Despite suffering heavy losses, Blücher withstood Napoleon's Grand Army at Quatre Bras on 16 June. Wellington fell back to Waterloo, to fields he had earlier identified as ideal terrain for his troops.

Not appreciating the care with which Wellington had planned his battle, Napoleon confidently launched his main attack at 1pm on 18 June, pounding the allied troops with a series of massive but uncoordinated assaults. Wellington paced the battle carefully, expecting the arrival of the Prussian forces late in the day. When they finally arrived in the early evening, Wellington still had 35,000 men standing; the French army was decisively routed. Napoleon withdrew to Paris, having lost about half his army, and abdicated four days later. For all the celebrations, Wellington knew that the Battle of Waterloo had been a very close call indeed. About 24,000 allied troops had fallen, alongside a French toll of 26,000 dead and another 10,000 missing. He famously wrote to a friend the following day: 'Next to a battle lost, the greatest misery is a battle gained.' The formation of his collections at Apsley House could be seen as a way of consolidating his victory in a personal museum, for he knew that Waterloo was 'the nearest run thing you ever saw in your life'.

*Top left: The Duchess of Wellington, in an engraving from a drawing by Sir Thomas Lawrence*
*Top right: Harriet Arbuthnot, in an engraving after a portrait by Sir Thomas Lawrence*
*Below: Giuseppina Grassini, the great Italian contralto singer and admirer of Wellington, shown here in a portrait by Ferdinando Quaglia*
*Below right: A fictional account of the adventures of the Duke of Wellington penned by the young, star-struck novelist Charlotte Brontë*

# The Ladies' Man

*Wellington attracted many female admirers, including two of Napoleon's former mistresses*

Throughout his life, Arthur Wellesley had a weakness for intimate conversation and correspondence with women that left him open to accusations of affairs, some of which were well-founded. Trim, 5ft 9in tall, with aquiline features (his large hooked nose caused him to be known to his troops as 'Old Nosey'), he had a way with words and many admirers. As his military career, spanning nearly 30 years, was spent abroad, he felt free to lead a bachelor life while Kitty raised their two sons in England. Unaffected and short-sighted, Kitty had none of the requisite skills of a society hostess and preferred to stay at their Hampshire home, where she could dress simply in muslin with no make-up. When she took to asking their servants about the duke's movements he warned her in writing, 'If it goes on I must live somewhere else.' Nevertheless, Kitty worshipped her hero from afar and they were reconciled by the time of her death at Apsley House in 1831.

Wellington's increasing celebrity only swelled his reputation as a ladies' man. During his residence in Paris after the fall of Napoleon, female admiration for Wellington became a craze known as *la nouvelle religion*. He is known to have escorted Napoleon's former mistress Giuseppina Grassini, and the French actress Mlle George, also a former lover of Napoleon, is reputed to have said that 'the duke was by far the more vigorous'. His principal female admirers in

London were Lady Jersey, Lady Shelley and Harriet Arbuthnot. They competed for his attention, a sport recorded in popular caricature engravings. Wellington admired Mrs Arbuthnot in particular for her social graces and her mind for politics. The unfounded tradition that they were lovers dates from the publication in 1887 of the diary of Charles Greville, who took revenge on the duke for having an affair in about 1820 with his mother, Lady Charlotte Greville.

Wellington's sincerest admiration was reserved for his elder daughter-in-law, Lady Douro, whose portrait hung prominently at Apsley House. Despite a lifetime of female adulation, he remained convinced that 'no woman ever loved me; never in my whole life'.

## WELLINGTONMANIA

After defeating Napoleon, Wellington returned to Paris as Commander of the Allied Armies of Occupation. Both Wellington and Napoleon were 46 years old when their military careers concluded at the Battle of Waterloo in 1815. Whereas Napoleon died in exile on the island of St Helena in 1821, aged 52, Wellington pursued a second career as a diplomat and statesman and remained in the public eye until his death in 1852, at the age of 83. More artists painted and sculpted Wellington than any other British sitter. Between 1795 and 1852 more than 200 likenesses were made by over 80 artists.

Wellington kept a pile of engravings of himself by his desk to send to admirers. The insatiable public demand also saw his portrait on cuff links, snuff boxes, brooches, mugs and even door stops. Wellington's distinctive appearance, however, was also used to less flattering purposes in numerous caricatures satirizing his political career.

## WELLINGTON THE POLITICIAN

In 1818 Wellington entered the Cabinet as Master-General of the Ordnance and ten years later reluctantly accepted the position of Prime Minister. In 1829 he successfully steered through the Catholic Emancipation Bill, allowing Catholics to be admitted to Parliament and to hold any civil or municipal office, as well as most Crown offices. Wellington's other foreign and domestic policies, however, increasingly showed that he was out of touch with the times, and his government fell in November 1830. His opposition to the Reform Bill, which aimed to redistribute votes to the expanding industrial cities, was supremely unpopular and led to riots in London, during which the windows of Apsley House were twice smashed by protesters. Wellington installed iron shutters and high iron railings to protect his town house, and it is thought that this may have led to his enduring nickname, the Iron Duke. The first published instance of the ever-popular sobriquet occurs in an 1842 edition of the satirical magazine *Punch*, which described Wellington as 'the Wrought-iron Duke'.

## FINAL YEARS

Wellington's final period in politics began in 1834 when he was returned as Foreign Secretary in Robert Peel's government. He was also appointed

The Master of the Ordnance Exercising his Hobby!

*Above:* Isaac Cruickshank's caricature of 1819 of Wellington as a ladies' man

*Left:* Wellington looking out of a broken window at Apsley House, which was attacked by protesters following his opposition to the Reform Bill. Wellington installed iron railings, which may have led to his nickname, the Iron Duke

*Below:* A caricature of 1830 by William Heath, showing the duke facing an angry mob outside Apsley House

THE REVIEW

GOING HOME TO GET THE BREAKFAST READY; the Jackall is the lion's surveyor — such of all Trades

*Right: The Duke of Wellington, painted by Francisco de Goya in just three weeks after the Battle of Salamanca (22 July 1812), in order that the portrait of the liberator of Spain could be shown at the annual exhibition of the Academia de San Fernando in Madrid. Goya managed this by painting Wellington's head onto a composition he had already begun, probably of Joseph Bonaparte*

'I lament the fate of having passed my Manhood acquiring celebrity; and of having to pass my old Age in sitting for Busts and Artists, that they may profit by it.' The Duke of Wellington, talking about the perils of celebrity, shown here in a portrait by John Simpson, c.1835

Chancellor of Oxford University in the same year. In the course of the following decade he held several important posts, including that of Commander-in-Chief of the army. He made a brief return to more active military duties in April 1848 when he was given responsibility for the defence of London, as Chartist rioting threatened to break out (although in the end this threat subsided).

Throughout this period, Wellington continued to demonstrate the conservative views that had lost him public support, but by the time of his death, at Walmer Castle on 14 September 1852, his popularity had returned in full measure. He was given a state funeral and buried in St Paul's Cathedral, taking his place in history as Britain's greatest military commander.

# Wellington at Home

*Wellington moved between houses, taking his own camp bed with him*

With his military career over, Wellington's lifestyle was less itinerant, but he still moved between his own houses, and those of his friends, in a way that was not unusual for a leading member of Regency society. Apsley House was never intended to be his year-round residence. Stratfield Saye in Hampshire was also acquired for Wellington in the same year. From January 1828 until November 1830, he served as Prime Minister and was able to live at 10 Downing Street while extending and remodelling Apsley House. From 1829, when he was appointed Lord Warden of the Cinque Ports, he also had the use of Walmer Castle on the Kent coast as his official residence.

## The Frequent House Guest

Until his wife's death in 1831, Wellington tended to avoid Stratfield Saye, complaining to his friend Mrs Arbuthnot that his wife 'made his house so dull that nobody would go to it'. He had to be in London for Parliament, which met from January or early February until July. Occasional excursions for house parties, fox-hunting and shooting peppered the London season, but by midsummer society removed to the countryside. In the autumn and winter Wellington would enjoy what he called 'a scamper about the country'. A regular house guest of Charles and Harriet Arbuthnot at Woodford Lodge in Northamptonshire, he once told his hosts that he regarded their house as his true home. On 7 September 1826 Mrs Arbuthnot noted in her journal, 'We are going to have a large

party, larger than the house will well hold, & the Duke (who is always the person that makes the fewest difficulties) brings his own little travelling bed.'

The contrast between the grandeur of the reception rooms at Apsley House and the modest apartments in which he really lived, not only in London but also at Stratfield Saye and Walmer Castle, suggests that the old soldier was not at home in society salons. Nevertheless, there certainly was a time when 'the Beau' liked to entertain in style. At Apsley House in particular he created palatial reception rooms where he could live up to public expectations of a duke, and of the conqueror of Europe.

TAKE UP YOUR BED - AND WALK !!!

# History of Apsley House

## THE SETTING

Apsley House stands on Piccadilly, at the formal entrance to Hyde Park. To the south and east lie Buckingham Palace, with its walled gardens, and Green Park. In the 18th century, following the expansion of London from the City, these parks formed the western boundary of Westminster. The location is recorded in a watercolour of 1756 (above), showing an apple stall at the park gates and an inn known as the Hercules Pillars. The location (according to Thomas Shepherd's popular guide *London in the Nineteenth Century*, published in 1829) was 'one of the finest in the metropolis, standing at the very beginning of the town, entering westward and commanding fine views of the parks, with the Surrey and Kent hills in the distance'. At the junction of Knightsbridge and Piccadilly a turnpike with toll houses, established in 1726, marked the end of the open land surrounding the rural village of Kensington and the entry into the capital. The first of the houses on the north side of Piccadilly consequently became known as 'No. 1 London' (its actual address today is 149 Piccadilly).

## THE FIRST HOUSE

The area grew fashionable with the development of Mayfair in the 1770s. Henry Bathurst (1714–94), who became Lord Chancellor and Baron Apsley in 1771, commissioned the architect Robert Adam (1728–92) to design and build Apsley House here the same year. By 1775, Henry had succeeded his father as 2nd Earl Bathurst, and acquired most of the land he needed for the house and its grounds through several Crown leases. Tradition holds that Bathurst forgot to buy out an apple seller, a widow named Mrs Allen (perhaps the woman in the 1756 watercolour), whose husband had built a cottage next to their stall. Allen's son claimed that the plot had been granted to his father by King George II for serving at the Battle of Dettingen (1743), and Bathurst only succeeded in buying the land in 1784. The brick-built house was completed at a cost of £10,000 in 1778, the year Bathurst left office. He is best known for building Apsley House: according to *The Oxford Dictionary of National Biography*, 'his abilities were mediocre and unsuited to the high offices which he came to fill'.

*Above: Reconstruction drawing of the house in 1817 when Wellington bought it from his elder brother, Richard Wellesley*

**1** The house built for Earl Bathurst between 1775 and 1778 by Robert Adam

**2** Turnpike toll gates

**3** St George's Hospital

**4** Hyde Park

**5** Green Park

**6** Piccadilly

*Right: A section through Apsley House from front to back, by Robert Adam, 1771, shows the original screened staircase and the extent of the cellars*

*Left: Robert Adam's design for the Portico Drawing Room ceiling at Apsley House, 6 April 1775*

*Below: Henry Bathurst, 1st Baron Apsley, in his Lord Chancellor's robes, painted by Nathaniel Dance. Bathurst commissioned the architect Robert Adam to build Apsley House in 1771*

Apsley House is one of only three large central London houses both designed and furnished by Robert Adam (the others being 20 St James's Square, 1771–5, and Shelburne House, Berkeley Square, about 1762–7). Sir John Soane's Museum holds 59 of Adam's drawings for Apsley House, dated between 1771 and 1779. In 1778 Adam also produced a series of designs for a gateway to London at Hyde Park Corner, including a toll house, weighbridge and pedestrian arches flanking the central road arch, with statues of the king and queen in niches. This grandiose structure would have stood west of Apsley House, but it was never constructed.

The house as built by Adam was recorded, in about 1818, on three dessert plates in the collection (see page 24). These sources and Adam's original plan record a five-bay house, set back behind a forecourt with a small lodge at the west end. To the east, blank walls rose above a stable yard. To fit the irregular site Adam built an oval staircase, lit from above and screened by two columns from the passage that linked the entrance hall to the dining room at the back of the house; a private staircase directly opposite led to bedrooms on the second floor. Beyond lay the dining parlour with an octagonal dressing room, a closet, service stairs and a garden entrance filling the gap behind the stables. On the west side of the house was a library and a large drawing room. Upstairs, Adam provided a suite of three drawing rooms and a bedroom.

## THE WELLESLEYS ARRIVE

Henry, 3rd Earl Bathurst (1762–1834), inherited the house from his father in 1794. A survey completed for him in 1796 records the stabling facilities to the east of the house: 'Stable yard three Coach-houses and Stables for nine Horses, with Servants Rooms over them'. In 1807, the 3rd Earl sold the lease of Apsley House for £16,000 to Wellington's older brother, Richard, Marquess Wellesley (1760–1842). Wellesley had been

*Right: View of Hyde Park Corner in about 1809, showing the turnpike gates with Apsley House on the left, by George Underwood*
*Below: Portrait of Hyacinthe Gabrielle-Roland by Elisabeth-Louise Vigée Le Brun, 1791. Hyacinthe was later Wellington's sister-in-law. She refused to leave Apsley House after she separated from Wellington's older brother, Richard, Marquess Wellesley*

dismissed as Governor General of India, and he had arrived back in England in 1806. Over the next two years he spent more than £20,000 on new furniture and decorative schemes at Apsley House, eventually moving into the house in 1808 with his French wife, Hyacinthe Gabrielle-Roland, and their children. It was not an auspicious move: dreadful scenes ensued and the couple separated. Hyacinthe refused to leave Apsley House and Wellesley embarked on numerous affairs. In 1809 he went to Seville as Ambassador Extraordinary, returning to London – and his love affairs – as Foreign Secretary in 1810. In 1812, on the assassination of Spencer Perceval, Wellesley attempted to form a government, but was too unpopular to achieve it; he lost office and incurred substantial debts.

Partly to alleviate his brother's debts, in 1817 Wellington put in an anonymous offer to buy Apsley House for the generous sum of £40,000. Wellington had just returned from Paris where he had served in turn as Ambassador to the Court of France and as Commander of the Allied Armies of Occupation. For some of this time he had been living in the Palais Borghese, which still serves as the British Embassy in Paris today. Wellington had bought the palace from Napoleon's sister Pauline, and now he needed a fashionable London town house to match.

## WATERLOO PALACE

When he acquired Apsley House, Wellington did not have any grand plans to renovate it, as he was expected to commission a magnificent new Waterloo Palace. The house and estate at Stratfield Saye in Hampshire were bought in 1817 to be the site of the palace. Wellington's chosen architect for the project was Benjamin Dean Wyatt, but Wellington finally decided to limit future liabilities for himself and his heirs by expanding and remodelling Apsley House alone.

Wyatt's alterations to Apsley House were carried out in two main phases, almost a decade apart, and with quite a different feel to them. Between 1819 and 1820 Wyatt added a three-storey extension to the east, to provide a state dining room with new bedrooms and dressing rooms above and below. The annual Waterloo Banquet was held in this new dining room from 1820 until 1829.

This early work gives little indication of the full-blown Louis-revival style that Wyatt later developed for the Waterloo Gallery. The sober neo-Greek design of this early building campaign sought to sit comfortably alongside the earlier interiors of the original house. It has a masculine character appropriate to a military hero, in contrast to the more overtly princely pretensions of a decade later.

*Left: Apsley House in about 1853, as altered and enlarged by the 1st Duke of Wellington and Benjamin Dean Wyatt, overshadowed by the giant equestrian statue of Wellington opposite (see page 11); lithograph by Robert Carrick after a painting by Frank Dillon*

*Below: A fantasy of a new London palace for Wellington exhibited at the Royal Academy in 1816 by Joseph Gandy*

## A GRAND ADDITION

The opportunity for a second phase of improvements at Apsley arose with Wellington's appointment as Prime Minister in 1828, when he had the use of 10 Downing Street (the Waterloo Banquet was held there in 1829). Wyatt wrote to Wellington on 3 May 1828 with estimates for a new wing to the west of Apsley House, in which to house the vast Waterloo Gallery, with a bedroom, dressing room and sitting room below. This was to cost £14,000, with a further £4,000 estimated for encasing the house in Bath stone and adding the portico over the new front door. The solid wall and gates in front of the house were replaced at this time with the high wrought-iron screen and gates to provide security (the turnpike had been removed in 1825) and to accord with the new Hyde Park Screen, which had been built between 1824 and 1825 by Decimus Burton.

### Remodelling Apsley House

Wellington took the opportunity to make several other alterations while these refurbishments were taking place. The main staircase was remodelled and its column screens removed. A similar screen was also taken out of the Piccadilly Drawing Room. Wyatt simplified much of the original Adam decoration, removing painted roundels from the ceilings and replacing pastel colours with cream and gilt. He also introduced vast plate-glass mirrors to make the most of the light that remained after he had lost windows on the west side to build the

*Left:* The Waterloo Gallery
*Below:* The gilded overdoors in the Waterloo Gallery, designed by Mrs Arbuthnot

**Right:** *The three Siena marble chimney pieces in the Waterloo Gallery were originally intended for York House but were installed here after the Duke of York died in 1827 in debt*
**Below:** *Detail of one of the exotic, fire-breathing dragons in the fireplaces*

Waterloo Gallery. New furniture and furnishings were supplied by Thomas Dowbiggin & Co., with metalwork for the doors and the windows by J Bramah & Sons and plasterwork by Francisco Bernasconi and George Jackson & Sons.

The showpiece of these improvements was the Waterloo Gallery. This grand picture gallery had to be worthy of the masterpieces from the Spanish Royal Collection, by Correggio, Velázquez, Murillo, Rubens, Van Dyck and others, which King Ferdinand VII of Spain had allowed Wellington to keep. The gallery also had to impress visiting monarchs and function as the setting for the annual Waterloo Banquet. Since Benjamin Dean Wyatt's first series of alterations to Apsley House, his architectural style had moved on. Together with his brother, Matthew Cotes Wyatt (1777–1862), he had pioneered the introduction of the French revival style, known today as 'tous-les-Louis' (from its use of design elements dating from the reigns of Louis XIV, XV and XVI). Belvoir Castle,

Leicestershire, was remodelled on these lines by the two brothers in 1824, and Benjamin Dean Wyatt was commissioned the following year by the second son of King George III, the 'Grand Old' Duke of York, to create York House in London (subsequently renamed Lancaster House) to the same taste. Unfortunately the Duke of York died in 1827, hopelessly in debt to his builders, and although the new owner, the 2nd Marquess of Stafford, kept Wyatt on, he was no longer the chief architect. The Apsley House commission therefore came at a fortunate time for Wyatt, and he was able to continue where he had left off on his designs for a great gallery at York House.

## REVIVAL STYLE

The new Waterloo Gallery revived the splendour of King Louis XIV's palace at Versailles. The *Galerie des Glaces* there provided the inspiration for Wyatt's mirrored walls but offered no design source for his ceiling, for at Versailles it is covered in paintings, as if floating above walls of light. The optimum display of the oil paintings in the Waterloo Gallery, however, required daylight to enter the room from above, through the ceiling. Wyatt chose to place a cupola at the centre of the gallery, which he may have derived from a design for the ceiling of 'le grand salon du Palais Royal' published in Paris between 1744 and 1748 by Gilles-Marie Oppenord. To either side of the cupola, Wyatt designed ceilings of intersecting circles; these follow an ancient pattern from a mausoleum that Wyatt found reproduced in a book by Robert Wood, *A General View of the Ruins of Palmyra* (London 1756). The remainder of this expansive flat ceiling is made up of gilded plasterwork and glass panes, while the cove and cornice help to distribute the light into the room. Gilded putti flank six shields bearing the duke's coat of arms in the cove, and in each corner may be seen the badge and collar of the Order of the Garter. The walls were kept clear of decoration to afford maximum space for the duke's paintings, but the three royal portraits were given new carved picture frames in the French rococo revival style, supplied by the duke's frame maker, Thomas Temple & Son, probably to Wyatt's design. They rise above three Siena marble chimney pieces originally designed by Wyatt for York House.

*Left:* Rubens's portrait of the Infanta Ana Dorotea, daughter of Emperor Rudolf II, as a nun of the convent of Descalzas Reales, Madrid, 1628

*Below:* The Egg Dance: Peasants Merry-making in an Inn, *by Jan Steen, c.1674, one of a group of Dutch paintings bought by Wellington at auction in Paris, 1818*

*Bottom:* Large Ships and Boats in a Calm, *by Willem Van de Velde the Younger, c.1660*

*Far left, bottom:* St Rosalie Crowned with Roses by Two Angels, *by Sir Anthony Van Dyck, 1624*

*Above: A view of Piccadilly, with Apsley House and Hyde Park Screen on the left, by Thomas Shotter Boys, 1842*

*Below: Reconstruction drawing of Apsley House and its setting in 1846*

**1** The house, expanded and refaced, 1828–30

**2** Statue of Achilles, erected in 1822

**3** Hyde Park Screen, 1824–5

**4** Wellington Arch, 1827–8

**5** Equestrian statue of Wellington, 1846

**6** St George's Hospital

## FINAL EXPENSES

By November 1828 architect and client had fallen out over costs and Wellington's friend Mrs Arbuthnot stepped in, noting 'when his house is the admiration of all London … I shall consider the merit all due to me'. The final cost of the extension and alterations was to be about £64,000. The yellow silk hangings were finally fitted in the Waterloo Gallery in March 1830, despite protests from Mrs Arbuthnot (see page 15). Still not satisfied, Wellington wrote to Wyatt on 24 October 1830 to complain that 'windows, doors, curtains, window shutters etc should be made so as to open and that with ease, to keep out the weather, and the chimnies not to smoke'. As Mrs Arbuthnot noted, 'he said the shame and ridicule of being so cheated and imposed upon, and the having been led on to an expenditure which must ruin his family, made him quite miserable'. It is possible that Wellington originally planned to hang a series of large portraits in the Waterloo Gallery, rather than these small cabinet-sized paintings.

Wellington must have had enough of builders, for no further alterations were made to the house in his lifetime. The 2nd Duke introduced red damask in the gallery and the Minton mosaic floors and radiator covers in the entrance hall and inner hall, and moved the Museum to its present location to display his father's valuable collection to its best advantage. Thereafter the house was preserved with few alterations.

**Left:** *Engraving of the Duke of Wellington in his bedroom at Apsley House* **Below:** Portrait of Richard Ford, *after Antonio Chatelain, 1840. Ford visited Apsley in 1853* **Below left:** The Duke of Wellington Looking at a Bust of Napoleon, *by Charles Robert Leslie, c.1845*

# The Duke's Own Rooms

Extracts from Richard Ford's book *Apsley House and Walmer Castle* (London 1853)

'Near the fire are the chair in which the Duke sat when giving instructions, and the table at which, when alone or much pressed by business, he ate a hurried but hearty dinner …

  'The Duke's own room … bears the look of the well-garnished comfortable library of a man of business … In this his studio, all the tools and means of a consummate artist who knows the value of time were at hand: while all show and tinsel are absent … Everything in this workshop is calculated to insure quiet and exclude draughts; for the Duke, however hardy out of doors, was chilly and loved warmth when chained down to the daily desk. Within easy reach we see the books he most frequently consulted, chiefly historical.

  'One door in this library affords immediate access to his bed-room – if such a term may be given to a confined barrack bivouac, exposed to the draughts of seven openings, and with only a few chairs and a narrow single bed for furniture … Curtained indulgences and eider-down pillows had no charms for him, whose hard mattress was so narrow that all stretchings were impossible.

  'His dressing-room adjoins – a good large room, and well appointed with arm-chairs, wardrobes, and all the appliances for what the euphuists term the due 'performance of ablutions'. The Duke, scrupulously neat in his person, well knew the bracing benefits of cold water and vinegar used externally, and of iced water taken internally – long his sole beverage.'

*Right: The Waterloo Gallery, set up for the bicentennial Waterloo Banquet in 2015*
*Below: A pair of Wellington boots designed and worn by the 1st Duke of Wellington*
*Below right: The Waterloo Gallery under wraps in 1943 during the Second World War*

## WELLINGTON'S SHRINE

Through the generosity of Gerald Wellesley, 7th Duke of Wellington, and through the passage of the Wellington Museum Act in 1947, part of the house was converted for public use as a museum. Apsley House opened to visitors in 1952, the centenary of the death of the 1st Duke of Wellington. A noted architect and Surveyor of the King's Works of Art, the 7th Duke was an expert on his great-grandfather, the 1st Duke. He also served as a member of the Advisory Council of the Victoria and Albert Museum, as Chairman of Trustees of the National Gallery and as a Trustee of the Wallace Collection.

Between 1961 and 1962 Park Lane was diverted to Hyde Park Corner, prompting the demolition of the houses immediately to the east and thereby cutting Apsley House off from

Piccadilly. The forecourt coach house was demolished, the new east façade clad in Bath stone and the public underpasses were formed.

Much of the historic furniture belonging to Apsley House had not been accepted by the nation in 1947, to facilitate the use of some rooms as venues for government entertaining. A campaign to restore the interiors was launched in 1977 by the Department of Furniture and Woodwork at the Victoria and Albert Museum, and the resulting research, redecoration and redisplay of the collection between 1978 and 1982 set new standards for historic house interiors. Further restoration followed between 1992 and 1995. In 2004 responsibility for maintaining and opening Apsley House transferred from the Victoria and Albert Museum to English Heritage.

As the restoration continues, Apsley House regains the atmosphere of a London palace, as it was known by the monarchs, diplomats, soldiers and servants who visited, lived or worked there. Several works of art and furnishings not originally retained in the public rooms have been generously loaned for display by the Duke of Wellington's family, and can be appreciated in their original setting today. Eight fine rooms are now open to the public, while the 9th Duke of Wellington and his family still maintain their private apartments in the house. Meanwhile, the rich documentary and pictorial evidence that survives provides an exceptional record for this magnificent house.